Cougar: Lion of the Mountains

By Allan Fowler

Consultants

Linda Cornwell, Learning Resource Consultant,
Indiana Department of Education

Jan Jenner, Ph.D.

Children's Press®
A Division of Grolier Publishing
New York   London   Hong Kong   Sydney
Danbury, Connecticut

Visit Children's Press® on the Internet at:
http://publishing.grolier.com

Designer: Herman Adler Design Group
Photo Researcher: Caroline Anderson

Library of Congress Cataloging-in-Publication Data

Fowler, Allan.
    Cougar: lion of the mountains / by Allan Fowler.
        p. cm. – (Rookie read-about science)
    Includes index.
    Summary: Describes the physical characteristics, behavior, life cycle, and habitats
of the puma, which is also called the cougar or the mountain lion.
    ISBN 0-516-21207-9 (lib. bdg.)   0-516-26560-1 (pbk.)
    1. Pumas—Juvenile literature. [1. Pumas.] I. Titles. II. Series.
QL737.C23F68   1999   98-22046
599.75'24—dc21   CIP
                                                           AC

GROLIER
PUBLISHING

Do you know the
difference between
a mountain lion,
a puma, and a cougar?

Actually, there
is no difference.

"Cougar," "puma,"
and "mountain lion"
are just three names
for the same animal.

Cougars live only in the
Americas. They are found
as far north as Alaska,
and all the way down
to the southern end of
South America.

Cougars were once
common all across the
United States and Canada.

Today they live only in the
far west.

A cougar's fur is grayish or reddish tan. The tip of its long tail is dark brown.

There are patches of white on a cougar's face, throat, chest, and legs.

Cougars are members
of the cat family.

A lion in Kenya, Africa

They look sort of like female lions, but lions are much larger and live in Africa.

A female lion roaring

Cougars don't roar like
lions do. They howl or
growl, hiss or scream.

Cougars are not the largest
cats in the Americas.
Jaguars are a bit larger.

An adult male cougar
weighs about 200 pounds
(90 kg).

Female cougars are smaller. Some weigh less than 100 pounds (45 kg).

Female cougars can give
birth to as many as six cubs
at once, but they usually
have two to four at a time.

A cub opens its blue eyes
when it is about 8 days
old. Later, the eyes darken.

For the first few weeks, the cubs stay in the den and drink only mother's milk.

A cub's dark spots
disappear by the time
it is 1 year old.

Cubs stay with their
mother for up to 2 years.

A cougar lives by eating other animals.

The cougar is a
skilled hunter.

It has no trouble
climbing up trees or
crossing rocky ledges.

It can leap more
than 20 feet (6 m).

Most of the time a cougar
hunts alone. If it kills a
large animal, such as a
deer, the cougar can feed
on it for about a week.

Then the cougar hunts
for another victim.

If a cougar can't find
a deer, it will eat mice,
rabbits, or even birds.

Cougars usually stay
away from humans.

They almost never attack
people, but sometimes
they kill farm animals
for food.

That is the main reason
people hunt and shoot
cougars.

Cougars no longer live in as many places as they once did.

But in rough mountain areas—far from cities, towns, and farms—the cougar is still king.

It is the lion of
the mountains.

Words You Know

adult cougar

cougar cub

lion

jaguar

31

Index

About the Author

Allan Fowler is a freelance writer with a background in advertising. Born in New York, he lives in Chicago now and enjoys traveling.

Photo Credits

Photographs ©: ENP Images: 14, 15 (Michael Durham), 13, 31 bottom (Gerry Ellis); Kevin Schafer: 3, 5, 7, 11, 23, 30, 31 top right; Photo Researchers: 25 (Alan Carey), 21 (E. R. Degginger), 18 (Jeff Lepore), 10 (Jeff Lepore/National Audubon Society), 24 (Leonard Lee Rue III); Tony Stone Images: 29 (Daniel J. Cox), 12 (Ian Murphy); Visuals Unlimited: 4, 20 (Gerard & Buff Corsi), 16 (Beth Davidow), cover, 9, 17, 31 top left (R. Lindholm), 19 (Joe McDonald), 26 (Leonard Lee Rue III), 8 (Tom J. Ulrich).